19.95
12-18-02

Everything You Need to Know About *Organic Foods*

Organic foods have grown in popularity in recent years.

Everything You Need to Know About Organic Foods

Elisha Dunn-Georgiou

The Rosen Publishing Group, Inc.
New York

Dedicated to my wonderful husband, Moulay Ali Ait Si Mhamed

Published in 2002 by The Rosen Publishing Group, Inc.
29 East 21st Street, New York, NY 10010

Copyright © 2002 by The Rosen Publishing Group, Inc.

First Edition

All rights reserved. No part of this book may be reproduced in any form without permission in writing from the publisher, except by a reviewer.

Library of Congress Cataloging-in-Publication Data

Dunn-Georgiou, Elisha.
Everything you need to know about organic foods / by Elisha Dunn-Georgiou.
p. cm. — (The need to know library)
Includes bibliographical references and index.
Summary: Discusses the organic food movement and recent information about the United States Department of Agriculture's criteria for what defines an organic food.
ISBN 0-8239-3551-5 (library binding)
1. Natural foods—Juvenile literature. 2. Organic gardening—Juvenile literature. [1. Natural foods. 2. Organic gardening.] I. Title. II. Series.
TX369 .D86 2002
641.3'02—dc21
                                                            2001003789

Manufactured in the United States of America

Contents

	Introduction	6
Chapter 1	You Are What You Eat	8
Chapter 2	A Short History of Organic Agriculture	15
Chapter 3	The Science of Food	23
Chapter 4	Organic Farming and the Environment	38
Chapter 5	Living an Organic Lifestyle	44
	Glossary	56
	For More Information	58
	For Further Reading	61
	Index	62

Introduction

Eating organic foods has become a popular and healthy trend. The origin and production of food influences the way people choose what they eat, where they shop, and the restaurants they patronize. If you've ever been in a health-food store or have even been browsing the shelves of your local supermarket, you've probably seen the word "organic" on some of the products being sold. But what does that word really mean? You have most likely heard the word in science class, but isn't all food just food? Why do some foods get labeled organic when others do not?

As you read through this book, you will begin to understand what makes a food uniquely organic. You'll also learn about the history of organic foods and what

Introduction

eating organic food means to some people. You'll discover several methods to take the first steps toward eating organic food and adding organic products to your everyday meals. If you are serious about including organic foods in your diet, be sure to talk with your family about your choice. They might be affected by your decision, especially if some of their favorite products are suddenly replaced by others. You will find that making the decision to include organic foods in your diet is a choice that could positively affect your health and the environment at large.

Chapter 1

You Are What You Eat

For many people, once they start thinking about what they eat and where it comes from, it is only a matter of time before they start to think about the other products they use. In the United States, it is possible to eat, drink, and wear only organic products. There are even organic products with which to paint and decorate your home. Just like the choice of eating organically, choosing to live an organic lifestyle is for many people a commitment to their environment and their health. Search for other types of organic products that might be available at your local natural-foods store. These stores can also be a great resource for products other than food.

Organic food is grown without using any artificial pesticides or chemicals.

What Is Organic Food?

There is something about organic food that makes it different from the other foods in the store. When you see organic fruits and vegetables in your supermarket, they may not look as attractive as commercially produced products. Organic fruits and vegetables grow in many different shapes and sizes and sometimes have blemishes—natural variations that occur in nature. But, with all of the different foods in supermarkets today and all of their fancy packaging and advertising, it is sometimes difficult to tell if a product is really what it seems to be.

A crop duster sprays chemical pesticides on a field of snap beans.

When a food is given the label "organic," it means that it has been produced without the use of any artificial chemicals, fertilizers, or pesticides. The word "organic" refers to a natural or "earth-friendly" method of farming and producing food. This means that those foods, such as fruits and vegetables, will never be sprayed with chemicals to keep insects from eating them. Organic food is instead grown using methods of farming that are less harmful to the environment than conventional techniques that utilize different types of chemicals. Organic farming methods

You Are What You Eat

are designed to work with nature, not against it. There are many kinds of foods that can be labeled organic, including fruits and vegetables, grains, dairy products, and meat. There are even organic convenience foods, like hamburgers and ice cream. As with fruits and vegetables, organic convenience foods are made naturally and usually without additives such as food dyes and preservatives.

Because organic foods are grown and produced naturally, many people say they have a better, fresher taste than nonorganic foods. Because they do not contain any added artificial flavors, colors, preservatives, pesticides, or other chemicals, many people feel that organic foods are the healthiest foods to eat. Fortunately, the fast growth of the industry and consumer demand for pure foods has increased the availability of these products and is making them less and less expensive.

The Trend Toward All-Natural Foods

While the average person might be completely unaware of the ways in which science has assisted agriculture over the last decade, there are others who are a part of a huge subculture of organic food eaters, or the organic food movement. Some organizations are listed in the back of this book. Most have elaborate Web sites that list many published articles that state different viewpoints on subjects related to agriculture and food production. Respected nonprofit groups, such as the Pure Food Organization, are good starting places for those interested in learning more about organic foods and the efforts of people like you to keep them on supermarket shelves.

Statistics now report that more than half of the U.S. population wants to eat only organic agriculture, instead of food produced from today's biotech world, according to a 1997 poll conducted by the genetic engineering corporation Novartis. One of the reasons for this newfound interest may be because of the pesticide residue that remains on commercially produced fruits and vegetables, sometimes even after they have been vigorously washed. According to statistics compiled by the Environmental Working Group (EWG), a nonprofit organization committed to eliminating toxins from mass-produced foods, more than a quarter of a million American children ingest a combination of twenty different pesticides every single day. In fact, some of the worst unpeeled fruits to eat are apples and peaches because their skins are known to retain more chemicals than other produce. Other fruits that are commonly contaminated include raspberries, strawberries, and cantaloupe.

You Are What You Eat

Hard Facts

It is not surprising that some manufacturers and farmers would want you to believe that their foods are organic even if they are not. After all, who wouldn't be happy to learn that they were enjoying foods free of pesticides and herbicides? The truth is that there are fewer organic farms in the United States than you think. Of the nearly 89,000 acres of farmland under the control of the sixty-nine land grant universities (subsidized farms), only 151 acres of land are certified organic, according to purefood.org, a nonprofit organization that acts as a watchdog for the organic food movement.

Additionally, the *New York Times* reported in an article by David Barboza on June 10, 2001, that an average of 100 million acres of the world's farmlands are now planted with genetically altered crops. The trend in the United States, however, is toward downsizing those acres. According to the same article, the amount of genetically modified crops dropped from 33 percent in 1999 to just under 24 percent in 2001.

It is likely that most of the foods you eat are *not* organic. Just because something is grown on a farm or has a label stating that it does not contain any artificial flavors or preservatives, doesn't mean that it is truly pure. Any fruit or vegetable that is grown using even

Most animals that are raised for their meat are fed nonorganic food and given artificial hormones or antibiotics to stimulate their growth.

slight amounts of chemical pesticides or fertilizers is not an organic food. If you see fruits and vegetables in the supermarket, do not conclude that they are produced organically. If there is no sign or label saying the food is organic, most likely it isn't. Likewise, any meat that comes from animals that have been fed nonorganic food and given artificial hormones or antibiotics is not organic meat. Many packaged foods also claim to be all-natural, with no added artificial preservatives or other chemicals. While that might be true, it doesn't necessarily mean that these foods are organic. Any organic processed food must be made with only natural, organic ingredients.

Chapter 2
A Short History of Organic Agriculture

To understand the history of organic foods, it is important to know something about the history of agriculture. Throughout most of human history, people have grown food organically, without the use of artificial chemicals and pesticides. And, for most of that time, food was grown on small farms and sold by farmers in their local areas.

The Industrial Revolution

The American agriculture industry was in full swing in the early 1800s. At that time, most farms grew a variety of different crops and also raised animals. Some of these crops were used to feed the farm animals, and manure from the animals was used to fertilize the crops. These small farms were self-sufficient

Throughout history, food has been grown without artificial chemicals and pesticides. It has been grown on family farms and sold locally by farmers in their areas.

and used only natural methods to sustain production. Many of these methods changed with the development of farming machinery and the beginning of the Industrial Revolution, a period of time when hundreds of machines were invented or perfected that changed the production of both goods and services around the world.

During the late 1800s and early 1900s, many of these machines, some utilizing systems such as the internal combustion engine or the electric motor, were developed that allowed farmers to increase their efficiency as well as expand their production. They were able to grow crops in greater amounts and, consequently, sell

The development of machines enabled farmers to increase efficiency and expand food production.

more of those products. At the same time, many advances in farming machines were developed that affected the methods in which food was transported.

Until the 1800s, products had to be transported by horse and buggy. This made it difficult for farmers to sell products outside of their local areas. But with the manufacture of trains in the 1800s, and then cars and planes in the 1900s, the transportation of food became much faster and easier. In addition, the Industrial Revolution impacted the farming industry in yet another way: It was the beginning of the first widespread use of chemicals as an effective way of controlling insects and fertilizing the soil.

Organic Foods

The First Use of Agricultural Chemicals

Some of the earliest pesticides used in the United States included arsenic, DDT, and lead. We now know that these chemicals cause serious health problems. They contain toxins and known carcinogens—substances that are cancer-causing agents. All of them have been banned in the United States for farm use even though they prevent the infestation of certain insects, but they are still used in a few countries around the world.

Farmers discovered that they needed to be more efficient to stay competitive in the growing market and had to choose between growing crops or raising animals. Without animals on their farms, farmers lost their natural fertilizers, and the use of chemicals as fertilizers quickly became more popular. According to the United States Department of Agriculture (USDA), by 1895, the nation was already using 1,845,900 tons of commercial fertilizers per year. By 1929, that number had increased to nearly seven million tons annually. The use of chemicals, combined with improved farm machinery, better agricultural techniques, and advancements in refrigerated transportation, enabled farmers to produce more fruits and vegetables, and transport and sell them at an increased profit. Few people, however, realized the great danger posed by the increased use of chemical fertilizers to both humans and the environment.

Pesticides such as arsenic, DDT, and lead are dangerous chemicals that contain toxins and known carcinogens. They can cause serious health problems in people.

By the beginning of the twentieth century, there were several people, including John Muir, John James Audubon, and Joseph Le Conte, who spoke out about the dangers of these new farming practices. These people advocated a return to the methods of organic growing and producing foods without chemicals that had been used for centuries. They warned that the new farming techniques would lead to pollution, eventual loss of crops, and health problems for both animals and people. In the 1940s, a man named J. J. Rodale started a magazine called *Organic Gardening and Farming*. In doing so, he was the first person to use the word "organic" when describing the methods of naturally growing and

America's First "New Environmentalist": Rachel Carson

One of the first modern public-health advocates to raise questions and issues about the use of pesticides was the scientist and author Rachel Carson.

In 1962, she published a book called *Silent Spring*. She did so after noticing that many of the wild birds she studied were laying eggs with very thin shells. The shells were so fragile, in fact, that the baby birds were less likely to survive. Carson was afraid that if this continued, many of the wild birds would face certain extinction because they would no longer have the ability to reproduce.

> When Carson took a closer look at these birds, she discovered that all of them had large amounts of chemicals, namely DDT, in their bodies, causing them to produce such fragile eggs. Carson's book was an overnight sensation. It warned people that the chemicals being used to produce more foods were actually killing wildlife and harming human health. This time, many people listened, including the United States government, which banned the use of DDT and began examining farming methods more closely.

producing food. Although many people followed Rodale's ideas and tried to return to a more natural way of farming, the United States government continued to advocate the use of chemical fertilizers and pesticides. By the 1960s, DDT was one of the country's most popular agricultural insecticides. However, it was only one toxin, or toxic substance, in the estimated 300 million pounds of chemicals that were sprayed over the four million farms in the United States alone. DDT not only kills insects but also poses a potential health hazard to nearby wildlife.

Organic Foods

Although the United States government has banned the use of DDT, the use of other chemicals has skyrocketed. The world's use of chemical fertilizer, for example, increased more than 900 percent between 1950 and the mid 1980s, according to facts introduced in the book *Food: The Struggle to Sustain the Human Community* by Jake Goldberg. In fact, one of the main reasons that scientists began experimenting with genetically altered foods was to decrease the use of chemicals such as pesticides and fertilizers.

Since the publication of Rachel Carson's *Silent Spring* in the 1960s, many other people have gotten involved in the organic food movement. But even with the attention her book generated, organic foods were still considered alternative foods, and their producers continued to be thought of as trendsetting outsiders.

Chapter 3
The Science of Food

The interest in eating organic foods has grown recently for several reasons. Some of these reasons include concerns about genetic engineering in food production and about the ways in which foods are handled during that production. Still, only 15 percent of Americans are aware that the majority of supermarket foods already contain ingredients that were altered by scientific means. Most people have no idea that most of the foods they are eating every day are genetically engineered.

Organic Foods

Genetic Engineering

Maybe you have heard the term "genetic engineering" before and know that it has become a common practice in the commercial food industry. Genetic engineering is a new way in which conventional farmers are trying to increase production and make their crops safe from insects. Some of these crops were altered to release their own insecticides or to remain hearty after chemical treatments.

Generally speaking, the genetic modification of foods combines genes from one fruit, vegetable, or even animal, with that of another fruit, vegetable, or animal. Though these new plants may now be resistant to disease, no one knows if they will have any long-term effect on the environment or on the health of people who eat them. In many countries, these newly invented crops are called "Frankenfoods," since they were created in the laboratory and are considered by some to be unnatural.

Genetic engineering is the scientific process of modifying a living thing's DNA material, or introducing new DNA material into it. Usually these heritable alterations produce foods in a more predictable way, although there are many who argue against such scientific tampering.

The Science of Food

Richard Lewontin, a professor of genetics at Harvard University, has expressed his concern about some of the recent advances in biotechnology: "People can intervene and change the ecosystem, but there's no way of knowing what the effect will be to the environment." Others claim that genetically altering plants can make newer strains of harmful bacteria that are resistant to traditional antibiotics. Once the genetically altered food is ingested by humans, our bodies also become resistant to those antibiotics, making bacterial diseases harder to control.

In one case in 1989, genetic engineering was actually responsible for thirty-seven deaths and numerous people becoming sick from an illness called eosinophilia myalgia syndrome (EMS) before the Food and Drug Administration (FDA) removed a particular dietary supplement from store shelves. The supplement, which was imported from Japan, became contaminated during the process of DNA recombination. Although this case did not involve a food item being contaminated with bacteria, that situation is also not especially unlikely, according to some scientists and pure-food activists.

Organic Foods

Are Genetically Engineered Foods Dangerous?

Genetically engineered foods are in question because some were found to increase allergic reactions in people who ate them or plainly reduced their original nutritional value. In the majority of situations, genetically altered foods are not harmful.

Most people, however, are unaware that this plant material, once released into the environment, cannot be contained, recalled, or cleaned. Genetic changes will be passed along to all future generations of crops for an indefinite period once they are imposed by science. Therefore, in an effort to create foods that are resistant to pests, we are actually putting crops at risk every time science tampers with genetics.

For example, consider some of the recent controversies that have surrounded the commercial production of contaminated biotech seeds from the StarLink Company. Although they involved only crops that were being grown for animal consumption, the results were widespread. The spread of the contaminated seeds led to "extensive food recalls in the United States and Japan," according to Stephanie Strom, a writer for the *New York Times,* in an article from October 26, 2000. Once the seeds were transported by the wind, as happened in this case, very little could be done to control their spread.

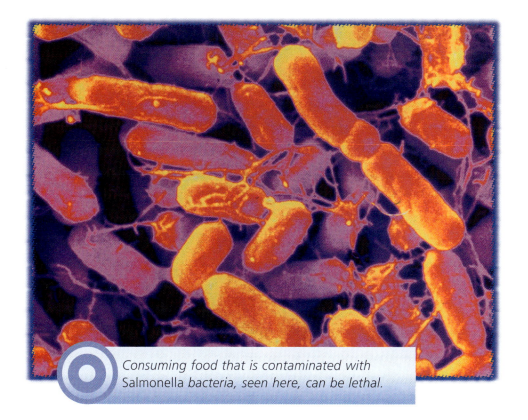

Consuming food that is contaminated with Salmonella bacteria, seen here, can be lethal.

Most scientists concede that since these altered crops have already entered commercial farming, consumers have little to no choice about consuming at least slight amounts of foods produced by the new biotech market.

Food Bacteria

Many people are concerned about the ways in which conventional foods are handled and packaged because of recent deadly outbreaks of *E. coli*, *Salmonella*, and *Listeria* bacteria. Contamination of this nature in

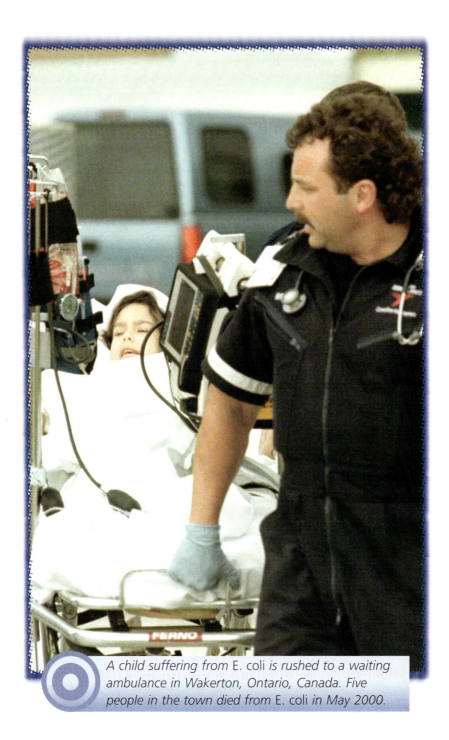

A child suffering from E. coli is rushed to a waiting ambulance in Wakerton, Ontario, Canada. Five people in the town died from E. coli in May 2000.

The Science of Food

mass-produced foods such as ground beef, cereal, and nonpasteurized milk and fruit juices are becoming the reason. The Centers for Disease Control (CDC) reports that there are at least 76 million cases of food poisoning every year in the United States alone. Some of these cases are linked to the production and manufacture of commercial foods in the United States and around the world.

In response to these concerns, and to an increased demand from consumers, more farms have been supplying mainstream supermarkets with organic products of all kinds. In fact, today organic food is the fastest growing sector of the food production industry. Because of increasing consumer awareness and concern over industrial farming methods, the United States Department of Agriculture has appointed a committee to ensure that all organic foods are certified using only standardized criteria and produced in a natural, environmentally friendly way.

Mad Cow Disease

Another concern is the recent outbreak of bovine spongiform encephalopathy (BSE), more commonly known as mad cow disease. The disease, which, as of this writing, has appeared in cattle mainly in England, Scotland, Ireland, and Portugal, has stemmed from the cattle being fed contaminated feed. The same malady, called Creutzfeldt-Jakob disease (CJD) when it appears

Many cattle farmers in the United States insist that their herds are safe from BSE, since using beef by-products in cattle feed is banned by the government.

The Science of Food

in the human body, is fatal to those who have eaten the contaminated beef products. It is a progressive brain disease that causes a slow wasting of the organ's tissue and is often difficult to diagnose and treat.

The actual disease is caused by a strain of mutated protein that enters the animal and multiplies. Unfortunately, doctors now think that the transmission of the disease occurred when animals were fed meal made from the ground up body parts of diseased animals. Now, animals thought to have this disease are being destroyed around the world.

The likelihood of developing such a disease is extremely rare, perhaps as rare as one case per billion servings of beef, as estimated by the European Commission on Food Safety. But the effects of the disease itself are horrifying enough for many to resist eating meat at all.

Setting New Standards

In an effort to set the record straight about which foods are all-natural, naturally produced, pure, or organic, the USDA recently passed a bill called the Organic Foods Production Act, in addition to its 1990 Farm Bill. The new law, which may take as long as eighteen months to become effective, forces farmers and commercial food producers to comply with rigid factors in order to label their foods as 100 percent organic. For fruits, vegetables,

Organic Foods

or grains to be certified according to the National Organic Standards Organization, harmful chemicals must not have been used on the farm for at least three years prior to the time of certification. Also, a certified organic farm must have yearly inspections and must keep detailed records of its farming practices. The new law mandates that certain substances must be avoided in order to farm organically and has set new rules for soil conservation and improvement. The approved bill, however, was not completely embraced by pure-food activists, who claimed that it was not specific enough.

"These are the strictest, most comprehensive organic standards in the world," explained U.S. agriculture secretary Dan Glickman during a February 2001 press conference to announce the new standards.

The new labels will read "USDA Organic," "100 Percent Organic," and "Made With Organic Ingredients." They are currently scheduled for adoption. These differences between labels and their language seem subtle and almost unclear, argue some. The "USDA Organic" label and the "Made With Organic Ingredients" label will appear on foods that are 95 percent pure, or less than 95 percent pure, respectively.

Some farmers who already grow 100 percent organic produce argue that the new rules offer loopholes where none existed before. "The administration of [the Farm Bill] is many steps backwards, and the rule itself is many

Ascorbic acid is used for canning fruit by food producers such as the Dole pineapple cannery, seen here.

steps backwards," argued Arthur Harvey, an organic blueberry farmer from Maine who also serves with the Organic Trade Association, a group that represents organic farmers. Harvey's concern was that the new bill does not address the ability of farmers who adhere to the standards only erratically. Another concern for activists is the accompanying United States government list of thirty-five synthetic additives, such as ascorbic acid and other food stabilizers, that are deemed organic by the new standards. (In most cases, ascorbic acid is a genetically modified chemical used only in the fruit industry for the purposes of canning.) Certainly, consumers and farmers alike have not heard the last of this discussion.

Antibiotics and Hormones

While the FDA approves of the increased use of antibiotics to treat animal disease on many commercial farms, pure-food activists and some scientists claim that their use could ultimately have an adverse effect on commercially prepared products. Items such as packaged beef, chicken, and pork products, as well as dairy products, including milk, cheese, yogurt, and ice cream, could have traces of antibiotics remaining in their contents stemming from the animal's original treatment. Some scientists are tying these antibiotic traces to a certain increased level of disease-resistant bacteria now seen in humans.

"It's not just a single pig or a single cow. It's a whole food commodity issue," stated Michael Osterholm, CEO of the Infection Control Advisory Network, when he explained information related to the use of antibiotics at a news conference in 1999.

Conclusions from a recent study at the University of Antwerp in Belgium found similar conclusions. "There is growing scientific evidence that the use of antibiotics in food animals leads to the development of resistant bacteria that can reach humans through the food chain," the study's authors concluded.

The Science of Food

Although proponents of antibiotic use claim that the studies are unfounded, they do suggest that farmers use these drugs as conservatively as possible.

Situations like this are further exacerbated when the U.S. government also allows the use of synthetic hormones, such as recombinant bovine growth hormone (rBGH), to boost the overall production of dairy products. As in the case of antibiotic treatments, pure-food activists insist that the use of rBGH is a trend toward a more chemically intensive, scientifically altered food supply.

What Is rBGH?

Recombinant bovine growth hormone is actually a genetically produced copy of a hormone already present in livestock. The approved use of milk procured from cattle that have been injected with a synthetic version of this hormone—rBGH—is useful to increase the milk production of each individual cow, but it has many side effects for animals and could have potential side effects for the humans who ingest it.

The question over the use of rBGH began shortly after its approval by the FDA back in 1994, when the government agency reported that its use had "no

Recombinant bovine growth hormone is an artificial copy of a livestock hormone. It may cause hormonal changes in those who drink milk that contains it.

The Science of Food

long-term effect on the health of consumers." Shortly thereafter, animal-rights activists and even FDA representatives claimed that its use could cause livestock to suffer from more infections, reproductive problems, digestive disorders, and other ailments such as tissue damage. Most of these conditions would also be treated with antibiotics, yet another reason for consumer concern. To fuel the fire, tests released four years after the FDA approved production of rBGH by its manufacturer, Monsanto, Inc., indicate the increased presence of cancer in laboratory mice that were also injected with regular amounts of rBGH over time.

Now, years later, rBGH is still in use across the country, although some companies—especially those that produce organic foods—have vowed to use only milk from untreated cows. As a result of increased public demand, other similar companies now include written statements directly on their products. One company that does this is Ben and Jerry's, Inc., the popular ice-cream producer from Vermont. Still, not every state allows food to be labeled this way.

Chapter 4
Organic Farming and the Environment

Unlike most conventional farmers, who seek to produce the most abundant crops that they can without much concern for the long-term environmental effects, an organic farmer's main goal is to keep the environment as sustainable as possible over time. This is not to say that organic farmers do not want to produce large amounts of produce or raise a variety of livestock.

Organic farmers know that they do not have to sacrifice their environmental concerns to increase production. The success of organic farming over the centuries has shown that it is very possible to protect the environment and produce abundantly at the same time. Organic farmers believe that these two ideas go hand in hand, and they use methods that work in relationship to

Organic farmers often prefer using natural fertilizers, such as manure, for growing organic foods.

one another to maintain their farms. Some of these methods include planting certain crops that work in conjunction with one another to control pests, practicing crop rotation, and using only natural fertilizers.

Because organic farmers do not use chemicals to control the land, they must search for creative solutions each year to adapt to the changes in their farm's soil. One of the main ways organic farmers work in harmony with nature is to rotate where they plant certain crops, where animals are kept, and the types of soil that are used to further enrich their plants. This means that, unlike conventional farmers, who plant the same crops year after year until the soil is

Rather than using herbicides to control the weeds growing around his grapevines, this farmer mows them.

depleted of its nutrients, organic farmers move their crops around every five to seven years to help keep the soil rich and fertile.

Organic farmers believe that pests can be kept under control by letting their natural predators eat them. For example, certain types of birds eat many of the insects that might be dangerous to a farmer's crops. If these birds have a comfortable environment to live in near the farm, they will take care of most of the troublesome insects without the farmer ever having to resort to using chemicals. The different crops that he or she plants, and the lack of artificial pesticides and fertilizers, make a

This organic farmer moves his free-range chickens so they can feed on insects and weeds.

welcoming home for an increased amount of natural predators, making pests less of a problem.

Farmers who also raise animals organically are careful to keep different types together and to move their placement every few years. This practice helps prevent the spread of disease and limits the need for the animals to take unnecessary medicines like antibiotics, which could ultimately remain in the food they provide, such as in cow's milk. On conventional farms, only the same type of animals are kept together, and they are often given large doses of antibiotics to help control the spread of disease.

Organic Foods

Controlling Pollution

Pollution is another reason many farmers choose to farm organically. Conventional farms produce tons of pollution each year in the form of greenhouse gases (dioxides that decrease the ozone layer) and contaminants such as pesticides that are released into local water supplies. This pollution also comes from the animal-raising practices on large farms.

Organic farming minimizes this pollution by banning the use of chemical pesticides and practicing recycling and conservation as much as possible. Organic farming also prohibits the use of the toxic sewage sludge that is sometimes spread on commercial farmlands. By mixing different kinds of crops and animals, organic farms are self-contained and limit their waste. For example, an organic farmer who raises cows and grows corn can use the manure from his cows to fertilize the soil for his corn crop. Likewise, the same farmer can use some of the corn he grows to feed his cows. By contrast, a conventional farmer would most likely raise only cows or grow only corn, as is done on most of today's large-scale commercial farms. The excess from these farms is considered waste and is often left to rot on small areas of land, which ruins the soil and creates additional pollution. To prepare this ruined soil for planting, the conventional farmer must use chemical

Organic Farming and the Environment

fertilizers. This process in turn creates more pollution and starts a cycle that is difficult to stop. Organic farming limits this cycle by taking care of the soil and animals through conservation and replenishment.

Farmers all over the world realize the need for organic farming practices. Organic standards vary from country to country, but all generally consider food organic if it has been produced without artificial chemicals. You can find organic farms anywhere on the planet.

Chapter 5
Living an Organic Lifestyle

People sometimes choose to eat organically for reasons that have little to do with their own personal health. These reasons may include a desire to replenish the environment, a concern for the safety and well-being of animals, or a commitment to keeping the economy stronger by supporting local farmers.

Some people choose organic foods because they believe that conventional farming damages the environment. Grazing the same animals or raising the same crops year after year can cause environmental problems, depleting the soil of nutrients and eventually causing soil erosion.

There has been more and more talk these days about the unethical treatment of animals used for tests by medical researchers, the fashion industry, and cosmetics companies. You've probably seen animal-rights activists

Support for the humane treatment of animals has led many to quit eating meat and using products tested on animals.

Organic Foods

protesting against the ways in which people use animals to test all sorts of products. Many people eat pure foods because they feel that organic farmers treat animals more humanely. For example, animals on an organic farm are allowed to roam freely within a controlled area. Farmers refer to these animals as "free-range" animals.

Often, on large commercial farms, animals are crammed together in small spaces and overcrowded stalls. Animals are not allowed to roam freely and some are in cages so small that they can not even turn around. Conventional farm animals are frequently given antibiotics to prevent disease and hormones to make them grow larger and faster than they would normally. These drugs sometimes remain in their muscles and blood. When you eat meat that comes from a conventional farm animal, you may also ingest these chemicals. Many people choose to eat only organic meat because they are assured that the livestock is raised in more comfortable conditions and is never given artificial hormones or antibiotics.

Others make the decision to eat organic foods simply to support small farmers. For most of us, going to the supermarket means buying food that comes from all over the country or even all over the world, but local or small farms do not have that same capability. With the beginning of industrialized farming, products were

Animals on commercial farms frequently live in unsanitary and overcrowded conditions. They are often given hormones to grow and antibiotics to prevent disease.

transported quickly from coast to coast. This meant that whoever could produce goods at the lowest price won a spot at the market. Unfortunately, this practice has hurt many small farmers who can't compete with large commercial business farms that transport and sell products all over the country.

Some people choose to eat organically because of the fresh taste of pure foods. Just one bite from an organic apple or one taste of organic ice cream is enough to make them consider the switch. Because pure foods are made without the use of chemicals, they are often said to taste better, fresher, and even sweeter than those produced from large, commercial farms.

Organic Foods

Lastly, other reasons for choosing to eat organic foods include the influence of friends or family, or even the simple desire to try something new. You might be thinking about choosing to eat organic foods for a bunch of different reasons. Maybe you have some ideas of your own about why eating organic foods is meaningful. The important thing is to learn as much as you can and try different foods to see what you like.

Making the Switch

Eating organic foods doesn't mean you have to change your entire diet. You should experiment with a variety of different foods and try whatever you think you might enjoy. There are many different kinds of organic foods available, from basics like bread and milk to exotic fruits and delicious ice creams. The next time you go to your local grocery store, search for an organic food section, since most stores keep all organic products together. Because of all the attention being paid to these foods lately, many conventional companies are expanding their product lines to include them. Look for new organic foods by General Mills, Heinz, and the Mars companies. If your supermarket doesn't have an organic food section, check your neighborhood for a natural-food or health-food store for more of a variety.

You don't have to change your entire diet to switch to organic foods, but you might have to do some research to ensure that what you are eating is organic.

Organic Foods

Advocates for organic foods will quickly tell you that they are better for you or more nutritious than nonorganic foods. Although pure foods do not contain chemical pesticides or fertilizers and are processed without any artificial additives, there is no hard evidence that they have a higher nutritional value than regular foods. Organic food is potentially better for you, but there is nothing to say that eating an organic carrot will give you more vitamin A than a nonorganic carrot.

Organic Gardening

Once you've started eating organic foods, you might want to consider growing your own garden. This is one of the easiest ways to enjoy organic foods. You can plant anything you want, from flowers and vegetables to herbs and fruit. Starting a garden can be a good way to involve your entire family in your newfound interest.

Organic gardening has many of the same benefits as organic farming, only on a much smaller scale. It works with the environment, not against it. By gardening organically, you can be sure that you and your family are eating healthful food without chemicals. By starting an organic garden in your backyard, you will be encouraging birds and butterflies to come to your

Organic gardening enables people to grow healthful food without chemicals. These organic gardeners are mulching their garden with leaf compost.

neighborhood. You can also limit the amount of household garbage your family produces by using some of it as fertilizer (compost) for your garden. If you start a garden, you should also incorporate plantings that will support and attract wildlife. This will help to keep pests under control and will limit your need to use chemicals. If you must use a pesticide on your garden, look for an earth-friendly product at your local health-food store or garden center. These are also great places to get tips about growing food organically or to join an organic growing club.

These gardeners are creating a compost pile rich in natural nutrients to mix with the soil for their organic garden.

Living an Organic Lifestyle

The Basics

The most important part of gardening organically is making an effort to build a good foundation soil. An excellent method for gaining a strong, healthy soil is by mixing compost material with it. This composted waste matter (coffee grinds, egg shells, fruit and vegetable peels—any nonprotein kitchen scraps) may be mixed with fall leaves, grass clippings, dead plants, and shredded newspaper to make a rich soil suitable to grow healthy plantings. Normally, compost material is kept in a separate section of the garden where it may be rotated regularly to keep its elements mixed well. Usually, this material is added as needed to the garden's topsoil.

Some people may find it beneficial to test their soil before they begin planting to determine specific things such as its pH, or level of acidity or alkalinity. Usually, farmers test a small sample of their soil by mixing it with distilled water in a clean container and then dipping premade pH strips into that mixture, or using an electric pH meter. This level is expressed in numbers; usually a pH of seven is an indication of a strong, healthy soil. Your local nursery will probably be able to recommend natural additives such as bonemeal, greensand, or rock phosphates to add if your pH is out of balance. Typically, an ideal soil for organic gardening is dark in color, moist, and lumpy. Earthworms are also a good sign, as is a sweet smell.

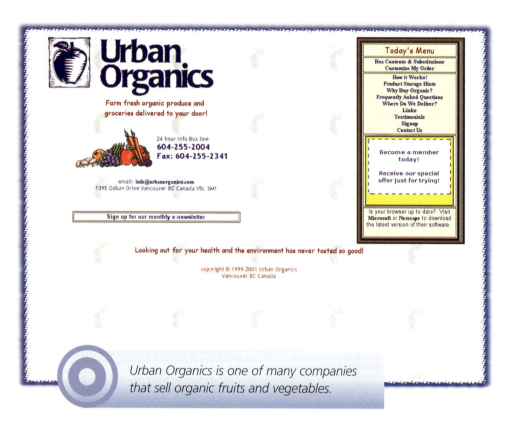

Urban Organics is one of many companies that sell organic fruits and vegetables.

The Future of Organic Foods

Now that you know a little about organic foods, you can see how easily they can be included in your life. As more people have become concerned about what they eat and how our food is made, the availability of organic foods has increased. The industry is now one of the fastest growing sections of the food sales market, and it doesn't show any signs of slowing down. This means that as more consumers desire pure food, more organic farms will be created. This is good news for the environment, since more land will be farmed without chemicals and there will be less pollution from conventional farms.

Living an Organic Lifestyle

Big businesses are also getting interested in organic foods because of the profits that the industry has been making. Many bigger food companies have been buying small organic companies. Even though this will increase the availability of organic foods, the interest of big business in this industry has many people worried. Pure-food advocates feel that big businesses are in it only for the profits and not for health concerns, for environmental reasons, or to support small farmers.

Businesses, consumers, and government agencies will have to work together to make sure that organic foods maintain the standards that have made them a healthy and environmentally safe choice for so many people over the years.

Glossary

activist Someone who takes a direct action to achieve a political or social reform.
advocate Someone who argues for a particular cause.
antibiotic Type of medicine used in humans and animals to help fight disease.
bacteria Class of microscopic, single-celled or non-cellular bodies that live in organic matter or the bodies of plants and animals.
compost Mixture of materials that consists largely of decayed matter and is used for fertilizing and conditioning soil.
conventional farm Large farming operation, sometimes owned by a corporation rather than an individual, that produces large amounts of farm goods.
DNA Deoxyribonucleic acid, the proteins that are the "building blocks" of life.

Glossary

fertilizer Substance used by farmers to help maintain soil balance in order to produce good, healthy crops. Fertilizers can be made from natural products such as manure or from man-made chemicals.

heritable Capable of being inherited or of passing by inheritance.

hormone Product of living cells that circulates in living tissue and produces a specific activity, such as regulating the tissue's development.

organic farm Farming operation that produces crops and/or raises animals using earth-friendly, chemical-free techniques.

pesticide Substance used by farmers and others to kill off insects that may harm crops or plant life. Pesticides are generally made from chemicals.

For More Information

In the United States

Environmental Working Group (EWG)
1718 Connecticut Avenue NW, Suite 600
Washington, DC 20009
(202) 667-6982
e-mail: info@ewg.org
Web site: http://www.ewg.org

Food and Drug Administration (FDA)
5600 Fishers Lane
Rockville, MD 20857-0001
(888) INFO-FDA (463-6332)
Web site: http://www.fda.gov

For More Information

Food Bytes, an electronic newsletter
e-mail: info@organicconsumers.org

Organic Alliance
400 Selby Avenue, Suite T
Saint Paul, MN 55102
(651) 265-3678
Web site: http://www.organic.org

Organic Consumers Association
6101 Cliff Estate Road
Little Marais, MN 55614
(218) 226-4164
Web site: http://www.purefood.org

The Organic Trade Association
P.O. Box 547
Greenfield, MA 01302
(413) 774-7511
e-mail: info@ota.com
Web site: http://www.ota.com

The Rodale Institute
611 Siegfriedale Road
Kutztown, PA 19530
(800) 823-6285
Web site: http://www.rodaleinstitute.org

Index

A
animal rights, 44–48
antibiotics, 14, 34–35, 37, 41, 46

B
bacteria, 27, 29, 34
Ben and Jerry's, Inc., 37
bovine spongiform encephalopathy, 29

C
carcinogens, 18
Carson, Rachel, 20–21, 22
Centers for Disease Control (CDC), 27
chemical fertilizers, 10, 13, 22, 40, 50
   history of, 18
   risks of, 19
compost, 53
Creutzfeldt-Jakob disease, 29

D
DDT, 18, 21–22
DNA, 24, 25

E
E. coli, 27

F
Farm Bill (1990), 31, 32
farming, 15–22, 38–43, 46–47
Food and Drug Administration (FDA), 25, 34, 35, 37
food poisoning, 27, 29
"Frankenfoods," 24

Index

G
genetic engineering, 13, 23–26
  defined, 24
  effects of, 24–25, 26

H
health-food stores, 6, 8, 48
herbicides, 13
hormones, 14, 34–35, 37

I
Industrial Revolution, 15–17

L
Listeria, 27

M
mad cow disease, 29

O
organic farming, 10–11, 13, 32–33, 38–43
  benefits of, 42–43
  techniques, 38–41
organic foods, 6–7
  defined, 9–11
  future of, 54–55
  history of, 15–22
  labeling of, 14, 32, 37
  movement, 11–12, 22, 25
  reasons for eating, 44–48
  recognizing, 13–14
  statistics on, 12, 13
  types of, 48
Organic Foods Production Act, 31–33
organic gardening, 50–53

P
pesticides, 10, 12, 13, 15, 40, 50, 51
  history of, 18–19, 21–22
  risks of, 19
pH levels, 53
pollution, 42–43
preservatives, 13, 14

R
recombinant bovine growth hormone (rBGH), 35, 37
Rodale, J. J., 19

S
Salmonella, 27
Silent Spring, 20, 22
StarLink, 26

U
United States Department of Agriculture (USDA), 29, 31, 32

About the Author
Elisha Dunn-Georgiou lives in New York State with her husband and two cats. She has a master's degree in epidemiology and currently manages a public health program that provides breast cancer screenings and education for uninsured women.

Photo Credits
Cover © Bob Daemmrich/The Image Works, Inc.; p. 2 © Tomas del Amo/Index Stock Imagery; p. 9 © Nancy Richmond/The Image Works, Inc.; p. 10 © Joey Gardner/AP Wide World Photos/*Salisbury Daily Times*; p. 14 © Mark Antman/The Image Works, Inc.; p. 16 © Hulton/Archive; p. 17 © A.R. Coster/Hulton/Archive; p. 19 © Galen Rowell/Corbis; p. 20 © AP/Wide World Photos; p. 27 © Custom Medical Stock Photo, Inc.; p. 28 © Reuters New Media, Inc./Corbis; p. 30 © Paul Connors/AP Wide World Photos; p. 33 © James L. Amos/Corbis; p. 36 © James P. Blair/Corbis; p. 39 © Richard Hamilton Smith/Corbis; p. 40 © Ed Young/Corbis; p. 41 © Julian Carroll/AP Wide World Photos/*Northeast Mississippi Daily Journal*; p. 45 © William Plowman/AP Wide World Photos; p. 47 © Bruce Burkhardt/Corbis; p. 49 by Cindy Reiman; p. 51 © Peter Huzdak/The Image Works, Inc.; p. 52 © Frank Siteman/Index Stock Imagery; p. 54 © Urban Organics.com.

Series Design
Thomas Forget